Milet Publishing
Smallfields Cottage, Cox Green
Rudgwick, Horsham, West Sussex
RH12 3DE England
info@milet.com
www.milet.com
www.milet.co.uk

First English–French edition published by Milet Publishing in 2013

Copyright © Milet Publishing, 2013

ISBN 978 1 84059 776 9

Original Turkish text written by Erdem Seçmen
Translated to English by Alvin Parmar and adapted by Milet

Illustrated by Chris Dittopoulos
Designed by Christangelos Seferiadis

Printed and bound in Turkey by Ertem Matbaası

My Bilingual Book

Hearing
L'ouïe

English–French

Our ears are like our radar

Nos oreilles sont comme des radars

for hearing sounds from far.

qui nous permettent d'entendre les bruits de loin.

Our ears delight in hearing shouts of glee.

Nos oreilles aiment entendre les cris de joie.

I am happy for you, and you are happy for me.

Je suis content pour toi, et tu es content pour moi.

Do you hear that buzz? Oh no . . .

Entends-tu ce bourdonnement ? Oh non . . .

It's a mosquito!

C'est un moustique !

The sweet voice of my mother

La douce voix de ma maman

is a sound like no other.

ne ressemble à aucune autre.

Hearing is a very sensitive sense.

L'ouïe est un sens aigu.

We hear sounds and also silence.

Nous entendons les bruits, mais aussi le silence.

When there's too much noise,

Lorsqu'il y a trop de bruit,

it's hard to hear one voice.

il est difficile de percevoir une voix.

I hear the sound of propellers, so I know

J'entends le bruit d'hélices, donc je sais

it's a traffic helicopter, flying low.

que c'est un hélicoptère qui vole bas.

If we could listen to music all day long,

Si nous pouvions écouter de la musique toute la journée,

we would learn the words to every song!

nous connaîtrions les paroles de toutes les chansons !

Our ears are for hearing what's around us,

Nos oreilles nous permettent d'entendre ce qui nous entoure,

and also for listening to what's inside us.

mais aussi ce qui est en nous.

Morning brings a happy noise,

Le matin s'accompagne d'un bruit de joie,

the sound of birds chirping, singing their joys!

celui du gazouillis des oiseaux qui chantent de plaisir !